12 Weeks to the
Happy You

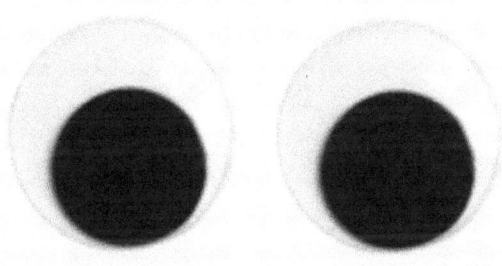

Workbook and Journal
Find Happiness and Inner Joy

Published in 2023 by Etheria Publishing

Table of Contents

Introduction

Week 1: Where Joy and Happiness Come From

Week 2: The Happiness Mindset

Week 3: Let Go of the Crap

Week 4: Forgiveness

Week 5: Embracing The Unique You

Week 6: Embrace Happiness

Week 7: Stay in Your Lane

Week 8: Get Creative

Week 9: Spreading Happiness

Week 10: Self Care

Week 11: Managing Stress and Anxiety

Week 12: Putting it All Together

Blank Journaling Pages

This book will help you understand what true happiness is to you and it will lead you down the path to finding and living it.

Wishing you joy and happiness in all of your days ahead.

-- M. A. Gallant

Find The Happy You

This journal was made so that it can be used alone.

But You will get the most out of it by using it along with "Find The Happy You."

Find the

Happy You

Buy Now

Find The **Happy You**

Discover the Happiness and Inner Joy You Desire

M. A. Gallant

If you haven't already, buy it now on Amazon by scanning this QR Code.

Week 1

Where Joy and Happiness Come From

What Does Happiness Mean to You?

As a starting point, write what happiness means to you. Don't think too much, just start writing.

Drink the Kool-Aid

The truth about happiness is that it is a conscious decision that anyone can make.

If you believe that you will never be happy, then you won't.

If you decide that you will be happy, then you can be.

Drink the Kool-aid. Make yourself believe that you can and will be happy.

Decide to be happy with fierce resolve.

Give yourself permission to be happy. Believe that you deserve it -- because you DO!

Starting today, tell yourself, "Today I will be happy."

At first, you might feel like it isn't doing anything, but keep telling yourself that every morning when you wake up.

This message will seep into your subconscious and you will start to believe it.

"Nothing can bring happiness but yourself" -- Ralph Waldo Emerson

Happiness is inside us all. It can't come from any outside source, because any feeling of happiness from outside of yourself is only temporary.

Happiness is your natural state. You were put here to be happy and enjoy this life. True lasting happiness happens when you are able to connect to that inner part of yourself and bring it out into your daily life.

The first step in connecting to the source of happiness inside you is to remember and experience the emotional sensation of happiness you have felt before.

Describe how happiness feels to you. Be as descriptive as possible.

Happiness feels:

_____

_____

_____

_____

_____

_____

_____

_____

_____

_____

_____

_____

_____

_____

_____

_____

Try this exercise:

Find a comfortable position, close your eyes, and try to bring the feelings that you described to your mind.

Let them flow through your body.

Sit for a moment and just experience what happiness feels like.

*"The most important thing is to enjoy your life -
to be happy. It's all that matters."*
- Audry Hepburn

List 5 things that make you happy.

1. _____

2. _____

3. _____

4. _____

5. _____

List 3 things you are thankful for

1. _____

2. _____

3. _____

Today, I am going to be happy!

What Do You Focus on?

What you focus on matters more than you think!

Do you give more time to bad news or good news?

Do you celebrate your wins or mourn your failures?

If your focus is more on the negatives than the positives in life, then you are doing yourself more harm than good.

There are many negative things that influence what we think about: the news, social media, the internet, and even the office busybody.

While you can't just shut out every negative thing that comes your way, you should put up a filter to control some of it.

If you spend too much time focusing on the bad rather than the good in life, then you need to make some changes.

Some suggestions:

 1. Limit the time you spend watching national news and true crime drama.

 2. Limit time spent with negative people.

 3. Unfollow social media connections that are always talking about negative things.

List some of the sources
of negativity in your life:

_____

_____

_____

_____

_____

_____

What thoughts come to your mind
when you experience these things?

_____

_____

_____

_____

_____

_____

Do this exercise:
Look over your lists.

Consider each thought you listed.

How do negative situations or people
affect your mindset? Do you feel
negative after being exposed to
negativity from others?

What can you do to prevent this?

What are the major sources of negativity in your life?

What can you do to limit or filter out some of the negative influences you are exposed to?

_____

_____

_____

_____

_____

_____

_____

_____

_____

_____

_____

_____

_____

_____

_____

_____

_____

_____

_____

_____

_____

_____

The way you speak to yourself is very important. When your inner voice is speaking down to you, it is your own brain bullying you.

It's important to remember that these things are seldom true at all. When you hear these thoughts in your head, you should question their validity and find ways to stop them or rephrase them into constructive thoughts that can be helpful instead.

Think about some of the negative thoughts that you experience.

"Life is too short to spend it
at war with yourself."
-- Unknown

I Will Not Take Any Crap From Myself

State the mean things you say to yourself

Do you believe that #1 is true? Why or why not?

Do you believe that #2 is true? Why or why not?

Do you believe that #3 is true? Why or why not?

What thoughts did you find that are valid and true? Why do you feel that these are valid thoughts?

_____
_____
_____
_____
_____
_____
_____
_____
_____
_____

Even negative feelings should be experienced and felt. What emotions do these cause in you?

_____
_____
_____
_____
_____
_____
_____
_____
_____
_____
_____

When you have negative thoughts about yourself, it can lower your self-esteem. Try to recognize these thoughts when they happen, then stop them by telling yourself "This is not a true or healthy thought." Then release that thought and imagine it floating away.

Describe 1 time when you caught and stopped a negative thought about yourself and how that made you feel.

_____
_____
_____
_____
_____
_____
_____
_____
_____
_____
_____
_____
_____
_____
_____
_____

Think of one time when your mind told you a lie that you believed. How did that affect you?

_____

_____

_____

_____

_____

_____

Did this lie cause you to do something that you regret?

_____

_____

_____

_____

_____

How did you react when you realized that your thoughts were not true?

_____

_____

_____

_____

_____

_____

3 Nice things that
happened this week

1. _____
2. _____
3. _____

3 Things that made me feel
proud this week

1. _____
2. _____
3. _____

3 Things I did that made me
happy this week

1. _____
2. _____
3. _____

3 Things that made me
smile this week

1. _____
2. _____
3. _____

Week 2

The Happiness Mindset

"Happiness is not something ready-made.
It comes from your own actions."
-- Dalai Lama

According to Sonja Lyubomirsky, Ph.D., of the
University of California, you have direct control
of 40% of the happiness you experience by doing
daily "happiness activities."

This journal will guide you through using some
"happiness activities" to jumpstart your mind to
feel happier.

These types of activities stimulate the brain to
secrete serotonin and endorphins - the "happy brain
chemicals." Once your brain starts getting a taste of
those, it will keep wanting more.

Weekly Goals

It's time to start establishing a habit of using goals with this journal. I will provide a few, and you can add a couple of your own.

Goals for You

1. I will complete all challenges in this chapter.

2. I will continue to use the tools learned in prior chapters

---

Goals Set by You

1. _____

2. _____

3. _____

Happy Mindset

Developing a Happy Mindset is the first step to finding happiness from within yourself. This week we will address Optimism, Enthusiasm, and Gratitude.

Optimism is an attitude. It means believing that things will work out, bad days will pass, and good things will happen.

Enthusiasm means to approach life with eagerness and enjoyment.

Gratitude means to focus your attention on being happy for what you do have, rather than being disappointed about what you don't have.

> You have survived every bad day
> you have ever had!
> - unknown

Optimism

If you broke your leg tomorrow, you wouldn't try to trick your brain into believing that it was actually a good thing, by telling yourself something like, "I'm glad this happened because now I will get the rest I've been needing." Denial is not healthy for you.

Being optimistic doesn't mean always turning a bad thing into a good thing, it is about accepting that bad things will happen, but seeing that it will not last forever.

The optimistic person would tell themself, "This is going to be a challenge, but I am going to follow my doctor's orders so that I can heal quickly and get my life back to normal."

The pessimist would say something like, "This is the worst thing that could ever happen!"

Happy people have an optimistic attitude about life. This helps them cope with life's hard times.

The good news is, if you aren't an optimistic person now, you can change that by paying attention to your thoughts and self-talk and adjusting the way you speak to yourself.

Is your glass half full?
Or is it half empty?

Do you consider yourself a more optimistic or pessimistic person?

Reflect on this for a moment, then write your feelings here.

Your Challenge:

During the next 24 hours, pay attention to your inner voice. When you notice a pessimistic thought, question it by asking, "Is this negative thought realistic?"

Then think about how you can changed that thought from pessimisic to optimistic.

At the end of the challenge, write your thoughts and feelings about this challenge here.

Enthusiasm

Enthusiasm adds spice to life. It is facing the world with excitement. It is taking an interest in everything around you. It is being eager and finding enjoyment in new things as well as the mundane.

People who are enthusiastic are happier and find more joy in life.

Did you know that you can cultivate enthusasm withine yourself? You can because it is a mindselt that can be developed.

You can work on developing enthusiasm by showing more intersst in the things you do everyday. Even if you have to fake it at first.

That's right - even when you fake enthusasim it sends signals to your brain that you are excited and energised. It sparks setatonen and endorphines in your brain, which trigger a boost in your mood, making you feel happier.

Because your brain responds this way, soon you will actually have a more enthusiastic attitude aobut things because your brain beginns to connect things you act enthusiastic about to getting a dose of the "happy brain chemicals."

Soon you will no longer be faking it.

Make a list of things you feel very enthusiastic about.

_____
_____
_____
_____
_____
_____
_____
_____
_____
_____

Describe thefeelings you have when you engage in these things.

_____
_____
_____
_____
_____
_____
_____
_____
_____
_____

Things you dread doing can be more enjoyable when you add a dose of enthusiasm to them.

What are your ideas about this concept?

What things do you think would be more enjoyable if you approached them with enthusiasm?

_____

_____

_____

_____

_____

_____

_____

_____

_____

_____

_____

_____

_____

_____

_____

_____

_____

_____

_____

_____

_____

_____

Your Challenge:

Try being intentionally enthusiastic about at least 3 things tomorrow.

Come back tomorrow and write about your experiences.

Gratitude

After firmly deciding to be happy, and taking full responsibility for your own happiness, the practice of gratitude is one of the most important things you can do to bring more happiness into your life.

A great way to start is by writing down 3 things you are grateful for each day. I want to do that now:

1. _____
2. _____
3. _____

Keeping a gratitude journal will help you stay focused on what you HAVE in your life, rather than focusing on what you DON'T have.

From here forward, each week, you will be provided with an area to write down 3 things you are grateful for.

This will help you stay optimistic and it causes your brain to produce the right chemicals to help you feel satisfaction and well-being.

Write your thoughts and feelings about practicing gratitude.

Do you feel that a daily gratitude practice will benefit you? Why or why not?

Will you commit to a daily or weekly gratitude practice?

_____

_____

_____

_____

_____

_____

_____

_____

_____

_____

_____

_____

_____

_____

_____

_____

_____

_____

_____

_____

3 Things
you are grateful
for this week:

_____
_____
_____

Who is
responsible for
your happiness?

Rate Your Happiness

1 2 3 4
5 6 7
8 9
10

What do you feel optimistic about?

_____
_____
_____
_____
_____
_____
_____
_____

How have you worked to change your optimism, enthusiasm, and gratitude?

How do you feel about your "happiness journey" so far?

_____

_____

_____

_____

_____

_____

_____

_____

_____

_____

_____

_____

_____

_____

_____

_____

_____

_____

_____

_____

_____

Week 3

Let Go of the Crap!

> *"Breathe in the good shit,*
> *breathe out the bullshit."*
> *—Karen Salmansohn*

Dealing with
Resentment and Anger

Holding onto resentment and anger only hurts you. It is impossible to find real happiness if you harbor these feelings, never letting them go.

Sometimes it seems like every day brings something to be angry about. Most of these are small slights, but of course, you will have situations when you become outraged, or resentful.

The best thing to do for yourself is to just let go of as many of these feelings as you can. And do it when they arise, without clinging to them.

I know, it can be much easier said than done.

This week is all about learning to explore the negative emotions that weigh you down and interfere with your daily happiness.

After understanding why you react in anger and hold resentment, you can learn to let go of these feelings so they don't continue to affect you down the road.

Think about the most recent time that you became angry. Write your thoughts and feelings about the situation.

Focus on how you felt in that moment and the thoughts you had.

_____

_____

_____

_____

_____

_____

_____

_____

_____

_____

_____

_____

_____

_____

_____

_____

_____

_____

_____

_____

_____

_____

Goals for this Week:

1. Practice working through feelings of anger and resentment.

2. Forgive someone who wronged you.

What is your venting style? Do you rage, or calmly express your anger?

_____

_____

_____

_____

_____

How do you handle confrontation?

_____

_____

_____

_____

Do you ever reflect on your feelings of anger?

_____

_____

_____

_____

Tips for Letting Go of Anger and Resentment:

When you release feelings of anger and resentment, you take back control of the power these feelings have over you.

It may sound hard, but you can do it. Start by thinking about what happened and the feelings you felt at that time. Ask yourself why you had those feelings. What does it trigger in you?

After you have identified these things, you can let them go.

Sit for a moment and give yourself permission to feel those feelings. Assure yourself that your feelings are valid.

Think about how these feelings continue to affect you.

Decide that you want to release those feelings for yourself, and no one else.

Close your eyes and take a deep breath. Bring the feelings back to mind and just sit with the feeling for another moment. Then give yourself permission to let them go.

When you exhale, imagine that the feelings are exiting your body and mind with your breath.

Time to practice:

Think of something you are hanging on to anger or resentment about. Try the releasing exercise. Start with something small.

Write about your experience. What did it feel like? Do you feel like it worked for you? Do you feel better

How You Vent Matters

Venting strong emotions can be a very healthy thing. You need to get some things off your chest sometimes.

What you may not realize is that the way you vent matters. Those who vent by unleashing full-on rage can actually do themselves more harm than good.

This style of venting intensifies the emotion and triggers your brain to focus on it more.

It is much more healthy to calm yourself, allow yourself to feel those emotions, reflect on them, and explore your thoughts and feelings.

Venting should be done after those things have happened when you can calmly express yourself without making the emotions even stronger.

Think of a time when you expressed anger with rage - shouting, spewing curse words, and waving your arm around.

Did it make you feel better? Did you find that those feelings lingered longer and stayed in your thoughts more?

_____

_____

_____

_____

_____

_____

_____

_____

_____

_____

_____

_____

_____

_____

_____

_____

_____

_____

_____

_____

Create a Few Goals of Your Own
Related to Anger management

1. _____
2. _____
3. _____

Just for today, I will be happy.

Do you feel better when you release anger?

Yes   No

Do you find it difficult to release anger? If so, are you committed to working on it until you can?

_____
_____
_____
_____
_____
_____

Another Tip for Releasing Anger or Resentment

Another way to release anger is to journal about it.

Try writing about what made you angry. Get it all out. Vent through your writing, allowing yourself to feel the emotions.

Write all your thoughts and feelings. Be sure to include telling yourself that your feelings are yours and you are allowed to feel the way you feel.

End your journal entry by giving yourself permission to let go of those feelings and be free from them.

Use the following page to write your journal entry.

Rate Your Level of Happiness

1 2 3 4 5 6 7 8 9 10

How well have you done with this week's goals? What are your thoughts?

_____
_____
_____
_____
_____
_____
_____
_____
_____

3 Things I am Grateful for This Week

_____
_____
_____

What Do You Feel Optimistic About?

_____
_____
_____
_____

Week 4

Forgiveness

> "Forgiveness does not exonerate the perpetrator. Forgiveness liberates the victim. It's a gift you give yourself." - T.D. Jakes

---

Forgiveness

Forgiveness can be a difficult thing, but it is an important part of finding happiness for yourself.

When you forgive someone, you don't do it for them, you do it for YOU.

Forgiveness allows you to let go of the feelings that hold you to the event that needs forgiven. It lifts a weight off your shoulders that is holding you back.

Forgiveness allows you to fully move on and let it go.

The art of forgiving requires you to explore the reasons you are holding on to a grudge. The answer will help you understand yourself more.

This insight is often very important because you are the only person in charge of your feelings.

When you take responsibility for your response to a situation, then you can change the way you feel and how you are affected by it.

People often describe the release felt when they forgive as "freeing."

Learn to free yourself by forgiving and letting go of the negative feelings you hold on to when you withhold forgiveness.

Week 4 Goals

1. Explore your feelings about forgiveness.

2. Forgive 1 thing or person.

3. Complete all tasks for this week.

What do you need to forgive?

_____

_____

_____

_____

_____

_____

_____

How do you feel about forgiving this?

_____

_____

_____

_____

_____

_____

_____

How Committed Are You?

Empathy and Compassion

Empathy and Compassion are the keys to forgiveness.

Empathy is trying to feel the way someone else feels by trying to see the situation from their perspective.

Compassion is being sympathetic to how someone else feels and what they experience or struggle with.

When you try to forgive, using empathy and compassion can help.

Can you understand how the other person felt? Try to explore things from their perspective. This doesn't mean condoning their actions but attempting to see what motivated them.

Once you try to see things from their side, whether right or wrong, try to feel compassion for what they were going through.

This may actually make it easy for you to forgive them.

Practice

Choose a grudge you are holding, and use empathy and compassion to forgive.

Write your thoughts and feelings while going through this exercise.

_____

_____

_____

_____

_____

_____

_____

_____

_____

_____

_____

_____

_____

_____

_____

_____

_____

_____

_____

_____

_____

_____

_____

Were you able to feel empathy?

Were you able to have compassion?

Were you able to find forgiveness?

Explore your feelings
about your answers.

_____
_____
_____
_____
_____
_____
_____
_____
_____
_____
_____
_____
_____
_____
_____

Forgive Yourself Too

I'm sure everyone has something in their past that they still feel guilty, upset, or disappointed about.

You must also forgive yourself for the things you're still beating yourself up over.

You deserve to be forgiven as much as anyone else.

What do you need self-forgiveness for?

Discuss it here along with how you plan to work through it and forgive yourself.

_____

_____

_____

_____

_____

_____

_____

_____

_____

_____

_____

_____

_____

_____

_____

_____

_____

_____

_____

Working on forgiveness is so important that I want to make sure you have plenty of opportunity to work through the things you need to forgive, whether it is someone else, or yourself.

So I am providing some pages for you to do just that.

Use them now or in the future.

How Optimistic Do You Feel This Week?

_____
_____
_____
_____

Today I AM Happy

3 Things I am Grateful For:

1. _____

2. _____

3. _____

Rate Your Happiness

1 2 3 4
5 6 7 8
9 10

Do You Forgive Easily?

Check Point

How is your happiness journey going so far? Are you continuing with the weekly tasks? What is going well, and where can you improve?

Week 5

Embracing
The Unique You

"Show the world your weird and wonderful side, for that is where true happiness is found."

- M. A. Gallant

Embrace Being Yourself

Truly being yourself all the time is the key to happiness. It is very hard to happy and untrue to yourself at the same time.

How often do you hide parts of yourself from others?

Do you worry about what others would think if they really knew how weird you are?

This is the furthest from the truth! Being yourself helps you find your tribe, those who fully love you for exactly who you are - not some fake persona that you put on show for the sake of others.

Being accepted for who you are at your core is so much more rewarding than making yourself acceptable to meet the expectations of someone else.

This week we are going to explore who you are and how you can proudly put that wonderful person on display.

This Week's Goals

1. Discover your truest self.

2. Practice letting people see you for who you are

3. Stop worrying about what others think of you.

Are you still working on your mindset?		Do you feel more optimistic?

Optimism
Enthusiasm
Gratitude

What are you happy about today?		What do you feel good about?

Set Your Own Goals

_____

_____

_____

_____

_____

Finding Your Authentic Self

Showing your authentic self to the World is a very important aspect of well-being and happiness. Yet it is something that many people struggle with.

Why? Because of fear. Do you fear being rejected or ridiculed? Being made an outcast, or thought of as a freak?

The first step is to stop worrying about what other people think and be determined to live for yourself.

First answer this: What do you hide about yourself and how does that make you feel?

_____

_____

_____

_____

_____

_____

_____

_____

_____

_____

_____

_____

_____

_____

_____

_____

Make a List of Things
That Make You Unique

_____

_____

_____

_____

_____

_____

How Many People See This Side of You?

_____

_____

_____

_____

Do You Show Your Unique
Side at Work or School?
Why or Why Not?

_____

_____

_____

_____

_____

How Do People Generally
React to This Side of You?

_____

_____

_____

_____

_____

Understanding who you are means knowing your best and worst traits.

List 5 things you love about yourself.

1. _____
2. _____
3. _____
4. _____
5. _____

List 5 things you dislike about yourself.

1. _____
2. _____
3. _____
4. _____
5. _____

What can you do to highlight your best traits?

_____
_____
_____
_____
_____
_____
_____
_____
_____

What can you do to improve upon your worst traits?

_____
_____
_____
_____
_____
_____
_____
_____
_____
_____
_____
_____
_____

Tips For Finding Your People

If you want to really connect with your tribe, then you have to find them.

Do you still collect rocks even though you're a full-grown adult?

Do you have a hobby that people consider "nerdy?"

Do you have a strange pet?

Get out there and find other like-mind wonderful people like yourself.

1. Join a club for people with the same hobby.

2. Take a class on something your interested in.

3. Attend events about something you enjoy and meet people there.

Here are some example:

- Photography classes
- Paint and sip classes
- Rock hounding club
- Quilting club
- Rock climbing clubs
- Craft fairs
- Attend a RomCon or ComaCon event
- Attend a Meet-Up

Your Challenge

This week, I challenge you to do two things:

1. Choose to show others your authentic self, even if it is little by little. Start now.

2. Attend one event where you can meet other people with similar interests as you.

Do You Accept?

YES!   NO!!

How will you meet this challenge?

_____

_____

_____

_____

_____

_____

_____

_____

Your Values

To be your authentic self, and ultimately be happy, your values and actions must align.

Circle the 5 values that most resonate with you. There are spaces to add your own if needed.

- Honesty
- Love
- Justice
- Loyalty
- Bravery
- Charity
- Integrity
- Fun
- Peace
- Humor
- Security
- Independence
- Hard Working
- Honor
- Adventure
- Knowledge

- Compassion
- Leadership
- Happiness
- Automomy
- Challange
- Community
- Faith
- Status
- Trust
- Creativity
- Health
- Stability
- Growth
- Wealth
- Service
- Respect

_____   _____   _____

_____   _____   _____

List the 5 values you chose here:

1. _____
2. _____
3. _____
4. _____
5. _____

How does your current life align with your values?

_____
_____
_____
_____
_____
_____
_____
_____
_____
_____
_____
_____
_____
_____
_____
_____

What are some changes you can make to align your life with your values?

_____
_____
_____
_____
_____

Did this chapter help you understand yourself better?

Yes!!   No!!

Do you feel more comfortable expressing your true self?

Yes!!   No!!

Did you take on the Challange? What did you learn?

_____
_____
_____
_____
_____

3 Things I am grateful for this week

_____

_____

_____

Something that made me happy was

_____

_____

_____

_____

I Feel Optimistic About

_____

_____

_____

_____

Rate Your Happiness

1 2 3 4 5
6 7 8 9 10

I Choose Happiness!

Week 6

Embrace Happiness

If it makes you happy...
DO IT!

Embracing happiness is all about doing
things that make you happy
... for the sheer joy of it.

That will be the focus of this week.

You will identify the things that just make
you feel good, and you will do them ...
often!

Ready?

Let's get started.

Week 6 Goals

1. Intentionally do something every day that makes you happy.

2. Learn how to stimulate your brain to make "happy chemicals."

3. Create a plan for doing "happy activities" weekly and monthly.

Happiness is a Choice Driven by Action

My Personal Goals

The Art of Intentional Happiness

Want to hear a little secret?

Intentionally planning to do things just for happiness brings... well, joy!

It isn't rocket science. When you set out to create happiness with intention, you are going to find it.

When you do things that make you happy, you trigger magic inside your brain. Things that make you feel good cause your brain to produce serotonin and dopamine.

Your brain loves these chemicals - it's basically addicted to them. As a matter of fact, these two chemicals are what cause people to become addicted to drugs, alcohol, gambling, and a lot of other things.

Why not become addicted to happiness?

Do you think that sounds strange? This phenomenon is backed by a lot of scientific studies.

When you do things that trigger serotonin and dopamine, your brain becomes energized, and you feel happiness. Your brain thrives on this feeling and it will start to drive you to do things that make you stimulate these chemicals over and over. That is how addiction works.

What if you could stimulate this reaction by doing fun things that bring you joy?

Trust me, it really is that simple. All you have to do is seek happiness and participate in activities that make you happy, and just like that you will feel happier, have more energy, smile more, and laugh more.

It's sort of life-changing.   Want to give it a try?

Make Lists of Things
That Make You Happy

3 Little Things That Make Me Happy
(things you can do every day)

1. _____
2. _____
3. _____

My Top 3 Happy Places
(places you could visit weekly)

1. _____
2. _____
3. _____

My Top 3 Happy Things to Do
(things you could do at least monthly)

1. _____
2. _____
3. _____

Do Something That Makes
You Happy Every Day!

Your Challenge:

From the prior page, do at least 3 things from one of your lists within the next 48 hours.

Write about your experience.

Give yourself permission to do things that make you happy - just for the joy of it.

For the rest of the week, your assignment is to do things every day that make you happy.

These can be things from the lists you made, but I also encourage you to be spontaneous. If an opportunity for fun pops up, take it!

Don't pressure yourself, but make sure you do one or two things daily - even if it is just a small pleasure.

I'm providing daily journal pages for you to reflect on and write about your experiences.

When you journal, focus on how you feel.

Explore your emotions, your overall feeling of happiness and well-being, and if you notice a change in your general behavior.

How Did Your Week Go?

Wonderful!   It was OK

Not so Great

How Optimistic Do You Feel?

_____

What Are You Grateful For?

_____

Which Was Your Favorite Day?

_____

Rate Your Happiness

1 2 3 4 5 6 7 8 9 10

Week 7

Stay in Your Lane

"What other people say about you is none of your business"
- Unknown

Sometimes the things people say can be hurtful, I know.

This is going to sound a bit harsh, but how it makes you feel is your responsibility.

That's right! If you feel hurt, disrespected, rejected, or anything else - you actually created that feeling.

If you've never heard that before, it can be hard to digest. How can the action of someone else be your fault?

It's not! - But your response is.

I hope you can take this to heart because if you can learn to live by this, you are going to be so much better off.

It comes down to this - you are responsible for your reaction to anything, including the opinions of others.

In other words, you decide how it makes you feel. You get to decide if you allow it to get in your head and ruin your day.

Or you can decide to simply move on, UNBOTHERED by it.

Week 7 Goals

1. Reflect on how you are responsible for your own feelings.

2. Practice taking control of your feelings and reactions.

My Gut Reaction to the Introduction

_____

_____

_____

_____

_____

_____

My Ow Week 7 Goals

_____

_____

_____

_____

_____

_____

Explore how you feel about being the one responsible for your feelings. Do you agree with this idea? Why or why not? If not, are you open to trying to understand and work on it?

Investigate Your Reaction

Taking responsibility for how you react to other people takes a bit of Mindfulness.

You need to explore your gut reaction and then consider why you reacted that way and if it is a valid reaction.

Then you can decide how you allow the situation to affect you.

Some factors to consider are how much you value this person's opinion. You may come to a different conclusion if it is a close friend, someone you respect, or someone you consider an enemy.

You will also take into consideration the intent of the other person. Are they trying to hurt you? Do they want to destroy your self-esteem?

Or, are they actually trying to be helpful?

Should your response be to just let it go, or should you try to do something differently?

Practice

Think of a situation when your feelings were hurt by someone's opinion of you.

Describe what happened.   Just the facts, please!

_____

_____

_____

_____

_____

_____

_____

Describe your initial reaction. What were your thoughts? What feelings did you experience?

_____

_____

_____

_____

_____

_____

_____

_____

_____

_____

_____

_____

Continue to the next page....

Why do you think you felt that way?

_____

_____

_____

_____

_____

_____

_____

What factors influenced your reaction? Who the person was? Where it happened? Other people present? Or something else?

_____

_____

_____

_____

_____

_____

If these things were different, would you have reacted the same way? Explain why.

_____

_____

_____

_____

_____

Keep going...

What was the other person's intent in saying what they said?

Be as objective as possible.

_____

_____

_____

_____

_____

_____

_____

Take a moment to reflect on what you have written so far.

Do you think you overreacted? Do you feel like your first response was valid? Why or why not?

_____

_____

_____

_____

_____

_____

_____

_____

_____

_____

_____

_____

Now Decide

After exploring the whole situation objectively, how would you choose to feel about it?

How different is this from your first reaction?

What will you do now?

Are you still practicing
the activities suggested
in prior chapters?

If you are, then you may be getting some feedback
on your actions from other people. Who's noticed
the new you?

Unfortunately, the world is full of sourpusses, so
you may also be getting some not-so-great
feedback.

Have you had a "backhand comment"? Someone
saying something nice like, "Well, aren't you a ball
of sunshine lately?" but in a sarcastic tone?

I hope you are moving on from those unbothered!

Challenge:

Be mindful of the things said to
you for the rest of the week and
decide how you want to react.

Use the next pages to journal
about your experiences.

How do you feel about this week?

Do you feel more in control of your feelings?

_____

_____

_____

_____

Something
I feel happy
about

_____

_____

_____

Something
I am grateful
for

_____

_____

_____

Something
I did just for
joy

_____

_____

Something
I am
optimistic
about

_____

_____

Rate your
happiness

1 2 3 4 5 6 7
8 9 10

Week 8

Get Creative

"Happiness is a byproduct of creativity. Create something and you will be happy."
— Osho Maitri

Creativity

Creative activities have a lot of benefits.

* They help you express yourself.

* They boost confidence.

* Creativity sparks the imagination.

* It stimulates the brain chemicals related to feelings of comfort and well-being.

* It helps with stress and anxiety.

You don't need to take my word for it, there is a lot of scientific research that backs up these claims.

If you don't have a creative outlet now, then you will find one this week.

Week 8 is all about being creative.

Week 8 Goals

1. Discover a couple of ways to be creative.

2. Develop a habit of creativity.

3. Participate in all activities.

List Some Ways You Are Creative

_____

_____

_____

_____

_____

_____

Your Week 8 Goals

_____

_____

_____

_____

_____

_____

Your Challenge

Do something creative at least 3 - 4 days this week. Try the prompts in this journal, or do your own thing. Either way, write about your experiences and how it made you feel.

Give yourself some bonus points if you try something new this week.

I am giving you an example of me trying something new. I made a coloring page for you. It isn't going to win any awards, but I did it.

Start your challenge by coloring my coloring page. I suggest using crayons or colored pencils because markers will bleed through the page.

Oh! And don't laugh at my artwork too much!

Actually, it's OK if you do! - At least I made you smile.

Creative Writing

Write anything, just write, as long as it is creative.

It can be a poem, short story, song, or a description of a fantasy landscape.

Floral Arrangement

Pick wildflowers, or go to a dollar store for some fake ones. Find a vase, jar, or bucket - any container will do. Create a floral arrangement for your home. If you want something a bit different, make a wreath instead.

If this really isn't your thing, come up with a creative project on your own and write about it here.

Create Your Own Drink

Get creative for your taste buds. Get some tasty ingredients and make your signature drink.

You can use the internet for inspiration, but it should be your own invention.

Write your recipe and how much you like it.

Try Something New

Try something you have never done before. What are you interested in, but have never done?

Maybe you try a Paint and Sip, or soap making, or photography class. You could also try your hand at pottery or crochet.

It doesn't matter what you do, as long as it is new to you.

What Was Your Favorite Activity? Why?

_____

_____

_____

_____

_____

What are you grateful for?

_____

_____

_____

Rate your happiness
1 2 3 4
5 6 7
8 9 10

What made you smile?

_____

_____

_____

What are you optimistic about?

_____

_____

_____

How did you spread happiness?

_____

_____

_____

What are you happy about?

_____

_____

_____

Checkpoint

At this point, you have spent 8 weeks working towards a happier you. This is a good time to reflect on your progress.

Think about the answers to these questions, then write a journal entry. I'm providing the next page to allow for plenty of writing space.

How do feel about the past 8 weeks of using this journal?

Do you notice a change in your level of optimism? Enthusiasm?   Compassion?   Gratitude?

 Have you noticed a change in your mindset?

How about your attitudes toward yourself and other people?

Are you actively working on the tips and suggested activities in this book?

What do you think you could improve? What are you doing well with?

Do you feel that your overall state of happiness and well-being are improved?

Week 9

Spreading Happiness

Happiness is contagious and you should infect as many people as you can!
                                        - M. A. Gallant

Spreading Happiness

Happiness is the best gift you can give someone else.

The funny thing is that it's a gift that comes back to you immediately.

Spreading happiness not only gives you a jolt of inner joy but also gives your brain a dose of those happy chemicals - serotonin, dopamine, and endorphins.

It doesn't have to be grandeur; just giving someone else a reason to smile is enough.

This week you will focus on spreading joy and happiness.

I encourage you to put all of your effort into this week's tasks. You will get a lot out of it if you do.

Week 9 Goals

1. Commit to participating in every activity presented in this chapter.

2. Reflect daily on how you feel when you spread joy to others.

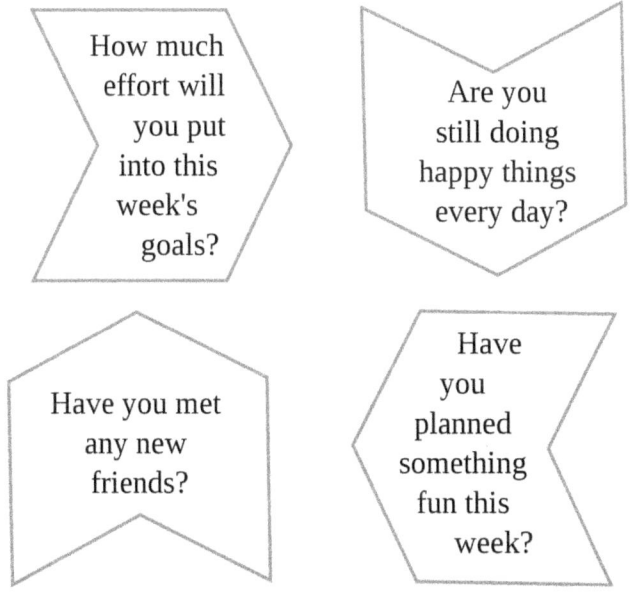

How much effort will you put into this week's goals?

Are you still doing happy things every day?

Have you met any new friends?

Have you planned something fun this week?

Set Your Own Goals

1. _____

_____

2. _____

_____

3. _____

_____

Start Small

The simplest way to help someone feel happy is to simply smile at them.

Your first task is to spend the next day smiling at everyone you meet: friends, acquaintances, and strangers.

Then come back here and record how your day went, focus on how you felt doing it.

Step It Up a Bit

I hope your day of spreading smiles was nice for you. I hope you got lots of smiles back, and it made you feel good.

The next step is making people feel good by giving small, but true, compliments. No BS allowed, that doesn't work the same.

On this day, whenever you speak to someone, mention a little thing that you like. It could be a compliment on their clothing, hair, perfume, or even their smile.

I know that sometimes this might be hard with some people you encounter. Make a game of coming up with something nice you can say about anyone.

I like to refer to this as "flirting with everyone." No, not in the conventional sense.

If you learn to do this, you will find that it is a pleasure to make everyone around you feel good about themselves for a moment. You might also find that you gain a few popularity points. People will see you as being nicer and more approachable. This is a handy advantage in many of life's circumstances.

Use the next page to record your experiences. Don't forget to explore your feelings about this activity.

Small Acts of Kindness

The next step on this path is to make yourself and others happy through small acts of kindness.

Yes, you can pay for someone's coffee in the drive-through, but there are so many other ways to do this:

* Let a car out in traffic
* Allow someone with only a few times to go ahead of you in the checkout line
* Bring a coworker a snack or drink
* Open a door for someone with their hands full
* Hold the elevator for someone
* Offer to help someone on a project
* Offer to babysit for a friend

The little things in life go a long way.

Your small act might make someone's day, or even be the help they really need.

Think about your daily life and make a list of small kindness acts you can do over the next few days.

_____
_____
_____
_____
_____

Continue spreading your smiles with everyone!

Keep making people feel good about themselves.

Your Challenge:

Spend the next 48 hours practicing everything from this week.

You have 2 journal pages for writing about your days.

How Well Have You Followed The Activities For Week 7?

_____

What made you happy this week?

_____

_____

How much did you enjoy Week 7?

_____

_____

How optimistic do you feel?

_____

_____

What are you grateful for?

_____

_____

Rate your happiness

1 2   3   4   5
6 7 8 9
10

Rate your enthusiasm

1 2   3   4   5
6 7 8 9
10

Spread Happiness
in a Big Way

Do you know that hundreds of thousands of people search Google for "How to be Happy" every month?

You may have even been one of them.

If this book is helping you, why not share it with others and help them find happiness too?

It's a small thing that can reach thousands of people.

Doesn't the thought of helping so many other people sound nice?

Simply scan the QR code to go to the Amazon page for this book and leave your review so others can find it as you did.

https://www.amazon.com/review/
create-review/?asin=9798866215607

Week 10

Self Care

> "How you love yourself is how you teach others to love you."
> — Rupi Kaur

Why Self Care is Not Selfish

You've probably heard it before, but how much effort do you really put into self-care?

Self-care isn't just about treating yourself to your favorite iced coffee anytime you want it.

It's about doing things to let yourself relax, de-stress and feel pampered. It's about treating yourself like the pampered princess (or prince) you are.

Self-care is an important step in your happiness journey because it helps you reconnect to yourself and treat yourself like you are important - because you are!

And you deserve it.

Self-care is about giving yourself what you really need. It's about loving and valuing yourself and your needs.

That is why Week 10 is all about self-care.

Week 10 Goals

1. Discover the true meaning of self-care.

2. Make a weekly plan for giving yourself love.

3. Stop feeling guilty for meeting your own needs.

What are your current thoughts and ideas about self-care?

_____

_____

_____

_____

_____

_____

_____

Set Your Own Goals

_____

_____

_____

_____

_____

True Self-Care

True self-care is about meeting your own needs.

Do you work too much and need some time off, but you feel bad about leaving your co-worker short-staffed?

Are you always there to help a friend out, even when you have things you need to do for yourself?

Do you stay up late working when you should go to bed?

These things are all easy to fall into. You don't want to let others down. Many of us do this even when it isn't the smartest thing for us.

Sometimes you must your own needs ahead of the wants of others.

Use the next page to explore the ways you neglect your own needs for the sake of others.

Think about what you wrote. How can you best meet your own needs?

_____

_____

_____

_____

_____

_____

_____

_____

_____

_____

_____

_____

_____

_____

_____

_____

_____

_____

_____

_____

_____

_____

Do you feel that you deserve to have your own needs met? Why or why not?

Be as honest with yourself as possible.

If the answer is "no" explore those thoughts and feelings, determine if they are true, then discuss that.

I am providing the next page for this as well.

Examples of Self-Care

* Taking a mental health day when you
  need it

* Enjoying a long walk on the beach

* Spending time with family

* A night out with friends

* Saying "no" to helping someone else when
  your priorities should come first

* A spa day

* Get a massage

* Go for a hike in a beautiful place

* Saying "no thank you" when offered over
  time that you really don't want it

* Spending a day in bed reading when you
  really need rest.

* Take a social media break

* Go on a scenic drive just for pleasure

* Use all your vacation time

Challenge

Give yourself some real love and self-care.

You don't have to do something from my list, but you can't do anything that costs money - unless it is paying for an activity (class, massage / spa day, event).

In other words - picking up an iced coffee or having your favorite dessert does not count.

Think bigger. Go all out for yourself!

I'm providing two pages to journal about your self-love action (or actions).

Make sure you include how it feels to love yourself and value your own needs.

How likely are you to continue practicing self-care on a regular basis?

_____

_____

_____

3 things I felt happy about

_____

_____

_____

3 things I feel optimistic about

_____

_____

_____

3 things I am grateful for

_____

_____

_____

Something I did to spread happiness

_____

_____

Rate your happiness

1 2 3 4 5
6 7 8 9 10

Week 11

Managing Stress and Anxiety

> "Today I will focus on
> stressing less and feeling blessed."
>
> - Unknown

Managing Stress and Anxiety

Every human experiences some level of stress and anxiety. It's natural. How you manage and respond when you are under stress or feel anxious is what matters.

Stress and anxiety are part of our built-in defense mechanism. They are meant to keep you safe in times of impending danger. Our cave-dwelling ancestors needed these mechanisms to keep them alert to the many physical dangers in their lives, and it helped them stay alive by activating the "flight or fight" response we all have.

Today, we still need these mechanisms to help us when we are in physical danger. Still, present-day humans also experience stress and anxiety from work or relationship pressure, emotional responses to the outside world, and pressures we place upon ourselves.

Managing stress and anxiety is an important aspect of finding your highest level of happiness.

Week 11 will focus on managing stress and anxiety.

Week 11 Goals

1. Identify your major sources of stress

2. Learn techniques for managing stress and anxiety

3. Discover 3 techniques that work best for you

Name 3-5 Sources of Stress or Anxiety

_____

_____

_____

_____

_____

Set Your Goals

_____

_____

_____

_____

_____

_____

_____

How Stress and Anxiety Affect You

Stress and anxiety have both physical and mental effects on you.

The physical symptoms include muscle tightness, shakey hands, headache, high blood pressure, and upset stomach. (plus more)

It gets worse when you are under stress or have anxiety for a long period of time. This can lead to developing ulcers, migraines, chronic inflammation, a lowered immune system, and an increased risk of heart disease.

The mental effects include mood swings, low self-esteem, excessive worry, poor focus, sleep issues, depression, and feelings of disorientation or brain fog.

In the long term, these can all get worse as well.

Use the journal prompts on the following pages to explore how stress and anxiety affect you physically and mentally.

Think about the last time you were under a lot of stress.

How did your body feel?

_____

_____

_____

_____

_____

_____

_____

_____

_____

What was happening in your mind?

_____

_____

_____

_____

_____

_____

_____

_____

_____

Think about the last time you felt very anxious.

How did your body feel?

_____

_____

_____

_____

_____

_____

_____

_____

_____

_____

What was going on in your mind?

_____

_____

_____

_____

_____

_____

_____

_____

_____

_____

Quick Techniques for Dealing With Stress and Anxiety

Insert a Pause and Breathe

When you start to feel overwhelmed simply stop what you are doing and focus on your breath.

Breathe in while counting to 4, hold for a count of 4, and then exhale to a count of 4.   Repeat as many times as needed to feel calm.

Five, Four, Three, Two, One

Sit somewhere and take a deep breath. Look around and find:

-5 things you see
-4 things you feel
-3 things you hear
-2 things you smell
-1 thing you taste

Muscle Relaxation

Find a quiet place where you can sit or lie down.

Start at your feet and relax each muscle group progressing up your body. Make sure to remember to relax your tummy, neck, and face.

Complete by going back down your body, relaxing anything that tightened back up.

(continued on next page)

Be Mindful of Your Thoughts

Stop and listen to your mind. What thoughts are you having?

Take a deep breath and change your thoughts to something helpful such as "I can handle this."

Get Moving

As soon as you can take a break, get outside if possible and take a walk.

Removing yourself from the current situation for a bit helps a lot, especially at work or school. If you can't go outside, walk to a different part of the building you are in.

Take a Musical Break

If the situation allows, pop in your earbuds and take a musical break.

This will both relax you and take your mind off things for a few minutes.

Get Physical

Hitting the gym is a great way to get relief from stress and anxiety.

If that's not your thing, try dancing, yoga, palates, or any other physical activity.

Challenge

Be ready for the next time you become overwhelmed by stress or anxiety. Then practice some of the quick techniques you just learned.

Fill out this page to help you be mentally ready then use the following pages to write about your experiences.

You can't always predict when stress and anxiety will pop up, so feel free to move on until the opportunity to try your techniques happens.

Just don't forget about it!

When do you need to manage your stress and anxiety the most?

Which techniques do you think will work best? Name at least 3.

Long Term Stress and Anxiety Management

The best way to keep stress and anxiety at bay is to manage it through daily management practices. You may notice that many of these were also listed when I talked about self-care. The two go hand-in-hand.

These include:

   -Getting plenty of exercise
   -Getting enough sleep
   -Regular relaxation practices
   -Practicing Mindfulness

When you work consciously to manage stress and anxiety, you will notice that stress decreases and anxiety doesn't have such a strong hold on you.

Your overall well-being and mental and physical health improve.

Long-Term Solutions

Long-term management of stress and anxiety is not a one-and-done thing. You must develop a routine that will help you keep things under control by taking care of yourself.

Some key things to focus on are exercise, sleep, relaxation, and mental health.

While you can't just do these things one time and call it done, you can begin your routine this week.

Exercise

If you want to be at the top of your game physically and mentally, you must put in some work. That means getting into a routine for exercise.

Regular exercise has been shown to not only make you feel better physically, it also improves mental health. It helps you get those happy hormones flowing, and it leaves you feeling self-satisfied. Exercise also gives you a mental break, because it's hard to worry or stress over your problems if you are doing a good workout.

People who exercise several times a week report less stress and anxiety, a better sense of well-being and they get many long-term health benefits as well. Routine exercise lowers your blood pressure and blood sugar levels, reduces your risk of heart disease, and gives you strong bones and muscles, which prevent injury.

It doesn't matter how you exercise, it's more important to find something you enjoy and can stick with.

Sleep

Are you getting the recommended 6-8 hours of sleep at night? If not, you should really try to.

Sleep is a time when the body and mind rest and rejuvenate. Many essential body functions happen while you sleep. Your organs get the rest they need. Your blood pressure lowers.

Your brain performs maintenance of sorts. Did you know that your memories form while you're sleeping? During sleep, your brain sorts through all of the day's events and selects what to put into short or long-term memory.

Brain hack: if you really want to remember something, just make a point of thinking about it right before going to sleep. This triggers the brain to put it in long-term memory.

When you don't get enough sleep, brain fog isn't the only consequence. People who don't sleep enough report having a harder time recalling things, they feel tired during the day, and they lack energy.

The effects of long-term sleep deprivation are similar to that of drinking too much. You can't focus, and you may become disoriented or confused.

What can you do?

Have a bedtime routine. Turn the lights down, take a warm bath, turn the TV off and read, or have a warm non-caffeine tea.

If you have a hard time at first, resist the urge to get out of bed. By remaining in bed even though you are not sleeping, you are telling your mind that it is time for sleep. With time, your mind will comply.

Relaxation

You need to take time to relax, preferably every day. Without taking time to relax, you become more susceptible to stress, anxiety, physical illness, and burnout.

Everyone has their favorite way to relax. Your personal choice doesn't matter, as long as it takes your mind away from your stressors and responsibilities for a bit.

What are your favorite ways to relax?

Mindfulness

I may have already slipped a little mindfulness into this book when I asked you to investigate your thoughts.

Mindfulness helps you deal with stress and anxiety by helping recognize your triggers and take control over them.

A good way to practice mindfulness is through meditation. There are many meditations specifically for mindfulness. You can find them on the internet, on YouTube, and in person in your local community. Look for shops that offer meditation classes.

Can you commit to changes?

What are your favorite ways to exercise?
When can you make time to exercise
3 times per week?

_____
_____
_____
_____
_____
_____

If you aren't sleeping enough,
what can you do to change that?

_____
_____
_____
_____

How can you incorporate a
little relaxation into every day?

_____
_____
_____
_____
_____
_____

How Do You Feel About Mindfulness?

Have you found the mindfulness work in this book helpful? Do watching your thoughts help you control your reactions? Will you seek more information about mindfulness or meditation?

Did You Use Any of the Quick Techniques for Stopping Stress and Anxiety?

_____
_____
_____
_____

What are you grateful for?

_____
_____

What made you smile this week?

_____
_____

How optimistic are you?

_____
_____

How is your stress level?

_____
_____
_____

How happy are you?

1 2 3 4 5
6 7 8 9 10

Week 12

Putting It All Together

> "Happiness is not something
> ready made.It comes
> from your own actions."
>
> — Dalai Lama

Putting It All Together

You've made to Week 12.

Congratulations on sticking it out. This journey has not always been a pleasant one.

If you have engaged in the exercises then you have challenged yourself, and your own mind. You have gotten outside of your comfort zone.

I hope you are happy with your progress so far.

The journey isn't over yet. You must keep going and keep pushing yourself to create the happy life you dream of. Because that is the only way you will get it.

This week you will take an assessment of how you have grown and transformed over the last 12 weeks.   You will also create a roadmap for where to go from here.

Ready to get started?

Reflection and Assessment

Spend a few moments thinking about where you were when you first picked up this book.

What made you buy it? What did you want from it?

Write your thoughts and feelings about that day.
Have you found what you wanted to find?

How do you feel now?
        (There is more space on the next page)

What part did you enjoy the most? Why?

What was the most difficult? Why?

Look at Your Progress

Go back through your journal starting with week 1. Fill in the graph below with your "Rate Your Happiness" scores.

Happiness Chart

S
C
O
R
E

10
9
8
7
6
5
4
3
2
1

1 2 3 4 5 6 7 8 9 10 11 12

WEEK

How do you feel about the results of your chart? Did you expect it? What attributed to it?

_____

_____

_____

_____

_____

_____

_____

_____

_____

_____

_____

_____

_____

_____

_____

_____

_____

_____

_____

Making Happiness a Habit

Happiness isn't something that necessarily just happens for everyone. Some were raised in a very pleasant environment which may have given them a headstart in this area. Others learn the right attitudes that lead to happiness even if they grew up with a lot of struggles.

Those people may not even realize that they "learned" to be happy.

I believe that happiness is a decision that you can make, but you must take action to see it actualize.

Do you agree?

The purpose of the past 11 weeks has been to give you the tools to develop happiness habits. These are actions you can take to spur happiness until it flows naturally for you.

It's up to you to follow through with this path. If you simply stop here, chances are good that your life will slowly go back to where you started before getting this workbook.

Take some time and review this journal. Are you regularly practicing the "happy habits" from the instructions? How do you plan to continue?

> "The best laid plans of
> mice and men often go awry."
> — Robert Burns

Staying On Track

Sometimes no matter how much you plan, life happens and things go sideways.

As you move down your path of happiness, you are still going to have challenges. You will have bad days.

You may even slip into depression, or fight anxiety.

I suggest you keep this journal and review it whenever you feel like things aren't quite on track.

I've put together a sheet of the main topics in this journal. You can cut it out and put it somewhere so that you can look over it from time to time. This will help you keep these happy actions close anytime you need to review them.

I've also placed many journal pages in the following the end of this week. I encourage you to use them as you go forward to help you stay mindful of your plan and your progress.

Happiness Actions

1. Give yourself permission to be happy.
2. Make happiness a choice - you decide.
3. Recall a happy time and bring back that feeling.
4. Focus on the good in life.
5. Practice gratitude daily.
6. Challenge negative thoughts. Are they true?
7. Be optimistic about life.
8. Count your happy moments.
9. Be enthusiastic in everything you do.
10. Speak to yourself like you would speak to a friend.
11. Let go of anger ASAP.
12. Practice compassion and empathy.
13. Forgive easily.
14. Always be authentically yourself.
15. Remember your personal values.
16. Do something that makes you happy every day.
17. Stay in your lane and mind your business.
18. Take full responsibility for your own emotions.
19. Self reflect often.
20. Stay connected to your creative side.
21. Share happiness with others.
22. Smile a lot.
23. Do something kind for someone else as often as possible.
24. Take care of yourself - mind, body and spirit.
25. Manage your stress and anxiety.

"Trust the next chapter, for you are the author."
                                    - Unknown

References

Achor, Shawn. The Happiness Advantage. First ed., Crown, 2018.

Black, Paula. "Forbes Councils Member." Forbes, Forbes Magazine, 05 02 2021, https://www.forbes.com/sites/forbescoachescouncil/2021/02/05/how-to-create-a-mindset-that leads-to-happiness/?sh=5f8cd32e392a. Accessed 22 07 2023.

Brooks, Arthur. "A Crucial Character Trait for Happiness." The Atlantic, 20 04 2023, \ https://www.theatlantic.com/family/archive/2023/04/enthusiasm-extroversion-big-five personality/673775/. Accessed 22 07 2023.

Christian, Lyn. "Defining Your List of Values and Beliefs (with 102 examples)." SoulSalt, 29 January 2020, https://soulsalt.com/list-of-values-and-beliefs/. Accessed 6 August 2023.

Drift. "7 Benefits of Traveling |DRIFT Travel Magazine." Drift Travel Magazine, 2023, https://drifttravel.com/7-benefits-of-traveling/. Accessed 3 September 2023.

Gallant, P. R. Un-Monkey Your Busy Mind: Reduce Stress and Anxiety. Etheria Publishing, 2023.

Legg, Timothy J. "What Are the Benefits of Sunlight?" Healthline, 2019, https://www.healthline.com/health/depression/benefits-sunlight#_noHeaderPrefixedContent. Accessed 22 August 2023.

Mayo Clinic. "Stress relief from laughter? It's no joke." Mayo Clinic, 20 07 2021, https://www.mayoclinic.org/healthy-lifestyle/stress-management/in-depth/stress-relief/art 20044456. Accessed 26 August 2023.

Mindful Communications and Such. "How to Manage Stress with Mindfulness and Meditation." Mindful.org, 2023, https://www.mindful.org/how-to-manage-stress-with-mindfulness-and meditation/. Accessed 26 August 2023.

Neff, MD, Kristin. "Self-Compassion." Self-Compassion.org, 2023, https://self-compassion.org/. Accessed 3 September 2023.

Robbins, Tony. "How to Find Yourself." Tony Robbins Personal Growth, 2023, https://www.tonyrobbins.com/personal-growth/how-to-find-yourself/. Accessed 06 08 2023.

Robbins, Tony. "12 Steps to Define the Purpose of Your Life | TonyRobbins." Tony Robbins, 2023, https://www.tonyrobbins.com/stories/date-with-destiny/what-is-my-purpose/. Accessed 27 August 2023

Scott, Steve. "54 Ways to Become a Happier Person." Happier Human, 30 March 2023, https://www.happierhuman.com/how-to-be-happy/. Accessed 15 August 2023.

Titova, Milla, and Kennon Sheldon. "Happiness comes from trying to make others feel good, rather than oneself." Journal of Positive Psychology, vol. 17, no. 10, 2021, pp. 1-15. Research Gate, https://www.researchgate.net/publication/349922479_Happiness_comes_from_ trying_to_make_ohers_feel_good_rather_than_oneself/. Accessed 15 08 2023.

Wooll, Maggie. "Start Finding Your Purpose and Unlock Your Best Life." BetterUp, 19 10 2021, https://www.betterup.com/blog/finding-purpose. Accessed 27 August 2023.

Yale. "The importance of relaxing Finding time to unwind." Being Well at Yale, July 2016, https://beingwell.yale.edu/sites/default/files/files/2016%20July%20Momentum%20Yale.pdf. Accessed 24 August 2023.